POINTS OF VIEW WITH PROFESSOR PEEKABOO

POINTS OF VIEW WITH PROFESSOR
Peekaboo

poems by
John Agard
Illustrations by Satoshi Kitamura

The Bodley Head
London

For my mother, Anna

1 3 5 7 9 10 8 6 4 2

Text copyright © John Agard 2000
Illustrations copyright © Satoshi Kitamura 2000

The rights of John Agard and Satoshi Kitamura to be identified as the author and
illustrator of this work has been asserted by them in accordance with the
Copyright, Designs, and Patent Act, 1988.

First published in Great Britain in hardback and paperback
in 2000 by The Bodley Head Children's Books
Random House, 20 Vauxhall Bridge Road, London SW1V 2SA

Random House Australia (Pty) Limited
20 Alfred Street, Milsons Point, Sydney
New South Wales 2061, Australia

Random House New Zealand Limited
18 Poland Street, Glenfield
Auckland 10, New Zealand

Random House South Africa (Pty) Limited
Endulini, 5A Jubilee Road,
Parktown 2193, South Africa

THE RANDOM HOUSE GROUP Limited Reg. No. 954009
www.randomhouse.co.uk

A CIP catalogue record for this book is
available from the British Library

ISBN 0 370 32623 7

Printed and bound in Hong Kong

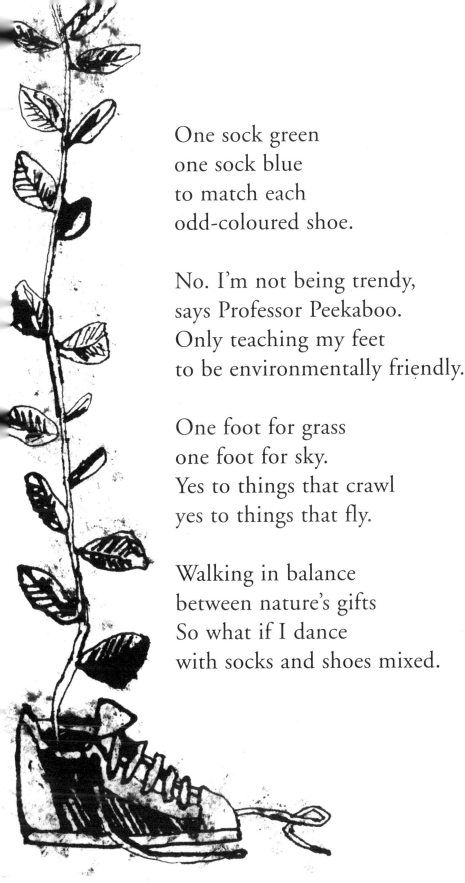

One sock green
one sock blue
to match each
odd-coloured shoe.

No. I'm not being trendy,
says Professor Peekaboo.
Only teaching my feet
to be environmentally friendly.

One foot for grass
one foot for sky.
Yes to things that crawl
yes to things that fly.

Walking in balance
between nature's gifts
So what if I dance
with socks and shoes mixed.

Fluent in many languages
such as Swahili and Urdu
not to mention Middle English
ancient Sanskrit, Latin, Hebrew.

But I really must brush up
on my Oink, Bow-Bow and Moo,
if I am to become a true
poly-lingual Peekaboo.

Once at a meeting with the Press
Professor Peekaboo out of the Blue
began hopping in public protest

Tell us briefly Professor Peekaboo
why an educated man like you
keeps hopping like a kangaroo?
Would you subscribe to the view
that you're essentially eccentric?

Allow me to stress to the Press
that life can be hellishly hectic.
If half the world had the hopping habit
there would be far less traffic.
Besides, hopping is non-toxic.

Next day the tabloid headlines read

PROFESSOR OF LINGUISTICS
IN ECO-HOPPING ANTICS

GRE
ARE

And quite vl
Or so Profess
As he peeked
and flah to
and sir all l
you from the
It's a silleas
Every man in t
we will the gu
that makes t
so when that r
so that a the
He seica got
Picture this a
Between then
saxophone and
Trumpet with
Piano plass

Litt
Gaps
WeT stone the
pres bone
yocacious b
nook and cr
that shelter
little sum e
that make
an eye it we
luno that be
to polish pla
with them

PROFESSOR OF LINGUISTICS IN ECO-HOPPING ANTICS

Once at the meeting with the Press Professor Peekaboo out of the blue beg
hopping in public protest. Tell us briefly Professor Peekaboo why an educated
man like you keeps hopping like a kangaroo Would you subscribe to the
view that you're essentially eccentric? Allow me to stress to the Press th

Green issues
are not to be treated lightly.
And quite rightly.

Or so Professor Peekaboo concluded
as he ponders forests denuded
and fish in rivers oil-slick-doomed
and air all laden with fumes.

So from his bed, he made a leap
and sat upon his compost heap.

Little gaps
in wet stone
that give home
to geranium

Little nooks
and crannies
that shelter
little fungi

Little seeds
of fern
that make an eye
in wonder turn

Little drops
that fall from sky
to polish plants
with dew

Thank you
little things
that enchant
the bigger view.

Vindaloo
Callaloo
Tofu
Foo Foo
Coo Coo
I love them all
says Peekaboo
but right now
what wouldn't I do
for a nice
cup of green tea
spiced with cinnamon
cardamon
almond
saffron
I can go
and on –
May tea follow me
to the great Beyond.

Was it you, little gene,
that caused Jack Sprat
to eat no fat
and his wife Mrs Sprat
to eat no lean?

Was it you, little gene,
that made that Johnny Green
put pussy down a well
and that Nellie Bligh
put a fly
in a hot mince pie?

Was it you, little gene,
little jumping gene?
Are you a gnome
within flesh and bone
or a genie that leaps
from the lamp of our deeds?

Speak now, little gene,
before it is too late
and a cow jumps over
the moon of my spoon
and a super-fish
runs away with my plate.

Why have two of Peekaboo
when one of Peekaboo would do?

No, thank you, I'll stay un-cloned.
Housed in singular flesh and bone.

But then again on second thoughts.
But then again on second thoughts.

Peekaboo one and Peekaboo two
could borrow each other's shoes

And argue on the telephone
about who's got whose chromosomes.

If bats
are batty

and loons
are loony

then in the name
of sanity

I'm proud to say
that I Peekaboo

am cuckoo.

Come sun
I will put on my shirt of saffron
and dance in light's honour

Come moon
I will wear my coat of dark velvet
and wave night's banner

for one brings rest
to the brain of Peekaboo
and one wakes him
with a birdcall to skyblue.

Sitting alone
on my throne
commonly known
as the loo

I Peekaboo
often ponder
the little things we humans do

like number one
and number two

Even kings and queens
who rule dominions
and moustached generals
who lead battalions

must do these deeds of privacy
memorised from infancy
and bow their bottoms
to nature's cue

of number one
and number two.

I'm singing
not in the rain
but under the shower.
I'm having my soap-rano hour

and it's against my ethics
to engage in tele-phonetics
when I Peekaboo
am in mid-shampoo.

Let the phone ring.
I'm indisposed.
I'm not at home.
My head *is* under a crown of foam.

If I perch
in a cage
am I a bird?

If I lie
on a page
am I a word?

If I hang
from a branch
am I a fruit?

If I hide
in the earth
am I a root?

O answers
are folly
when questions bring bliss

Without questions, can I exist?

When does a frog
gallop
instead of hop?

When does a frog
trot
and not squat?

Tell you what,
when a frog
is a pad
of tissue
under a horse's foot.

How about a new
high-stepping fashion
of rubber frog-cushions
under human feet?
Then we could be shoed
like horses

     and as we gallop
     in out trend-setting clogs
     we could ask each other

     how do you like my latest frog?

When you cross a camel with a llama
they say you end up with a cama –
a Bambi lookalike called Rama.
But will three wise men I ask ya –
following that star of wonder –
look any calmer on a cama?

Another scientific trump.
A camel with no hump.

Let the camel be striped
and the tiger be humped.

Let the parrot be spiked
and the hedgehog be feathered.

Let the armadillo be furred
and the rabbit be armoured.

Let the seals be ten-toed
and humans be flippered.

Then each can have a go
at being a bit of the other

And Peekaboo would insist
that feet-tending chiropodists

be now called flipperopodists.

It's such fun
to say tun-tun
the Chinook
word for heart

I often do
says Peekaboo
and roll my tongue
around the u

So let's get down
to the tun-tun
of the matter

Love someone
from the bottom
of your tun-tun

Distance makes
the tun-tun
grow fonder

Home is where
the tun-tun lies
Cross my tun-tun
and hope to die

O for a good
tun-tun
to tun-tun
conversation

Listen
to the throb
of your tun-tun

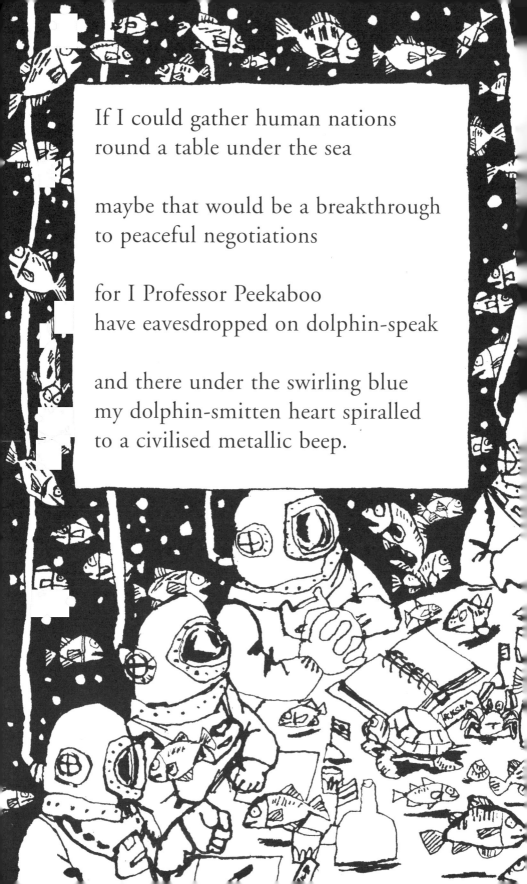

If I could gather human nations
round a table under the sea

maybe that would be a breakthrough
to peaceful negotiations

for I Professor Peekaboo
have eavesdropped on dolphin-speak

and there under the swirling blue
my dolphin-smitten heart spiralled
to a civilised metallic beep.

Round the reefs of Hawaii
there swims a tiny fish
called HUMOHHUMOKUNOKUAPUAA

But deeper into the deep
There swims a giant fish
called simply O

which only goes to show
Never judge the size of a fish
by the sound of its name

for in the game
of human conversation
when words stay dumb

one single O
can say enough to fill an ocean

I've studied a dog's bow-wow
and an owl's tu-wit-tu-wu

Recorded a cat's meow-meow
and a cock's cockle-doodle-doo.

Scribbled notes on a pig's oink-oink
and a cow's moo-moo

But how I long to know
sighed Professor Peekaboo

the extinct voice of one Dodo.

The black keys
always intrigued
Professor Peekaboo
who felt they were the clue
to the piano's mysteries.

You won't get far,
his music teacher advises.
You'll never be a Mozart
by leaving the white keys
to their own devices.

But Professor Peekaboo
even then a precocious child –
told his teacher with a smile.
Something tells me I have the knack
to compose Rhapsody in Black.

And true, said little Peekaboo,
there's a duet that I do
when a ghost comes out at night
and sits beside me on the stool.
This way I orbit black and white

and learn the key of midnight blue.

Professor Peekaboo
walked among the ruined
libraries of Timbuktu
but could not unlock the past.

Professor Peekaboo
felt among the bones
of owl and caribou
but could not foretell the future.

Neither book nor feather
neither dice nor bone
would surrender some fleeting clue
to the what's-new of the universe.

So peering through the midnight blue
at the planets' silent hullabaloo

Professor Peekaboo
pondered Martian matters
with the might
of his grey matter

Anwer me, night
How long does it take a human
to shatter
into blazing diamonds?

Somewhere a word wanders and weeps
for a mouth that no longer speaks.

So I'll probe all oblivion
for a single exclamation.

Armed with my vowel-o-metre
and consonant-detector

I'll scour caves for ancient whispers
and marshy ground for gutturals.

Where do they go, these fragments of
sounds
that once were spoken living tongues?

Let shine from majestic rubble
One splinter of a syllable.

O dead languages, come back to me,
plant in my throat your forgotten tree.

With my little eye
I Peekaboo spy
something that begins with

O

a kind of skin
that's wearing thin

a living shield
for everything that breathes

somewhere up there
in the upper air

for when the sun throws down
its ultra-violet spear

Is it Oxygen
        Ozone
                or Oblivion?

Oil slick, oil slick,
the sea is sick,
send for the doctor
quick-quick-quick.

Tell the siren-fish
to sound its alarm
Tell the drum-fish
to toll its drum

Ask what ails thee, Sea?

But no whales hum
No dolphins click

O what have we done?

Would you rather spend your cranium
in the splitting of uranium
to fashion a fission-bomb?

or would you rather break the tedium
in the discovery of helium
that makes a balloon rise and rise?

Peekaboo knows to whom
he'll give his Nobel Prize.

Why work yourself into a tantrum
when your yo-yo tangles on its string?

From my yo-yo studies I've learnt one
fact –
yo-yos respond
to words of encouragement and tact.
Let me have a go.

Say nice yo-yo
say up yo-yo
say down yo-yo

Repeat this to infinity
for according to Peekaboo's yo-yo
tantrum theory:

Familiarity with a yo-yo
breeds respect for the law of gravity.

A word with you, Mr. Biro,
inventor of the biro.
It's famously handy I know,
and I'd be the last to knock it.
But what force makes the ink flow
onto Peekaboo's pocket?

Before money took the form of silver
and notes
goods could be paid for in goats,
for cattle was currency stashed,
and rock salt was instant cash
as chocolate was Aztec tax.
Money you could say was edible.

These days people flash plastic
from a purse or a wallet,
which may be more flexible,
but when you're back of a queue
and feeling as peckish as Peekaboo
a wad of plastic isn't so digestible.

If on red nose day
I wear a green nose
instead of red
it's not because my nose
is colour-blind
or has been misled.

It's not to take my mind
away from childhood's time
when my nose sometimes bled.

No, it's just for a joke.
Today I'm a traffic light
and I'm telling green-fingered folk,
all guardians of seed
and things that grow

Proceed. Proceed.
Go right ahead,

When the train is late
some say this kind of thing
can infuriate.
Some say perhaps we ought
to agitate.
Some resign themselves
to their fate.
Mostly people just wait
for the indicator
to indicate.
At times like this says Peekaboo
I wish I could levitate.

Instead I simply close my eyes
and recall childhood's train-set days
when all the floor was my Waterloo
and there was no late running of
my choo-choo.

Some things we remember, some forget.

One worked copper into weapons
One worked copper into bracelets

One caused a bloody crisis
One brought relief to arthritis

Some things we remember, some forget.

One worked iron into swords
One worked iron into pots

One for hacking a fatal blow
One for cooking with fire low.

Some things we remember, some forget.

They stand to attention
for the wind's inspection

They take orders from the sun
and also obey the rain

They salute the skyline
and rustle their green bayonets

They often close ranks
but have no army tanks

They are only trees
as I am only Peekaboo

and their uniform is peace.

Eye-piece
for eye
that peers down the lens

nose-piece
for nose
of specs, ladies' or men's

ear-piece
for ear
that hears the dial tone

mouth-piece
for mouth
chatting down the phone

hair-piece
for hair
gone bald or straggly thin

head-piece
for head
when the battle begins

neck-piece
for neck
to snuggle into fur

but no heart-peace
for heart
in a warring old world

When put to the test
my computer beats me at chess
and hardly forgets.
Its memory is micro-fine

Remind me, says Peekaboo,
to teach this computer of mine
that to forget is divine.

MOONDAY
TUBEDAY
WEBDAY
THUNDERDAY
FRY-UPDAY
SATURNDAY
SAUNADAY

A relaxing end
to a busy week
says Peekaboo
MOONDAY will soon
be here again.